THE WHITE TAILED DEER

An introductory booklet for children

By

Martha Philbeck

Contact:

goldenpaws@embarqmail.com

I wish to express a special thank you to Marty and Sara Creech for letting me take pictures and the special contributions they made to make this book possible.

Several pictures were also from Frances Jennings. I have a field camera set up also to document the movement of deer in my woods.

Martha Philbeck

12/05/10   10:32 PM

goldenpaws@embarqmail.com

THE WHITE TAILED DEER

An introductory booklet for children

Starting life as Fawns

A female deer is called a doe. She gives birth to babies called fawns in May or June. They may have 1 to 3 at a time. The fawns coat is reddish brown with white spots. The spots are formed by white tipped hairs. The spots will disappear about 5 months when they molt or get their winter coat for the first time.

A doe leaves her fawns hidden in brush or tall grass while she eats. She may leave them up to 4 hours. For the first 2 weeks after being born, they have no scent to attract predators.

A baby will lay in the grass with his head out stretched and is practically invisible. The white spots also help to blend them in with nature.

They do not go to the bathroom until the mother comes back. When they go to the bathroom, she eats it so there is no sign of the fawn.

At birth the fawns weigh between 3 and 6 pounds. They can walk and follow their mother. She licks them dry after birth.

At birth they are weak and wobbly, but are up walking shortly after. This fawn is less than 24 hours old.

Within the week they can run. They start to eat vegetation a few days after birth.

They nurse for 5 weeks and then they are weaned about 6 weeks. Doe(s) come into heat in Nov. for 24 hours. Young does will usually have one fawn, while older does will have twins or triplets.

If they don't get bred they will come in again in 28 days. In about 200 days they will give birth. Females generally follow their mother for 2 years, but males leave the group the first year. They form transient groups of 2 to 4 in the summer and disband prior to the mating season.

This fawn is a month old. It is very alert and can already run fast. In captivity they are usually bottle fed to help tame them down for handling.

Bucks and does remain apart except during breeding season.

This fawn is 2 months old. The mother's milk is very rich and they grow fast.

This fawn is 4 months old and very alert. Notice the changes in size and how fast they are growing.

This is a front view of the 4 month old fawn. Notice the long slim body and slender legs that are made for speed.

Trails are the paths that deer travel. They are narrow and usually connect where the deer eats and where it rests.

Sometimes the paths cross and we call them super highways. You can tell they are well traveled by the lack of vegetation.

A deer bed is a pressed down spot about the size of a man in leaves, grass or snow.

This is what they call a piebald fawn. His white spots are not the same as the other deer. He has more white on him. Look at the hind legs, his side and the freckles on his nose.

Eyes

A white tailed deer has very good eyesight. The big eyes are located on the side of the head and allow the deer to see ahead and behind without moving its head. The oversize ears can hear incredibly well. They can also rotate like radar to pick up sounds. Their nose is wet and shiny and looks like patent (man-made imitation) leather. It looks like a black ceramic cup, you know how shinny they are. That is what a deer's nose looks like. By keeping it moist it increases the sense of smell.

Deer are virtually color blind, but they see shapes sharply and clearly and can detect the slightest movements. Their most developed senses are hearing, smell and sight.

Deer teeth

They are born with 4 baby teeth. In the next couple of months they develop baby incisors and pre molars. Deer are actually aged by their teeth and the wear on them. By the time they are 18 months old, permanent teeth will have replaced the baby teeth. At 1 year and 6 months old, deer start loosing their first three bottom side teeth or pre-molars. During the following month, three new permanent teeth will appear and replace these three baby teeth. The key to aging deer at this age is to look at the third tooth on the bottom.   If this tooth has three cusps it's a baby tooth and its age is 1 year and 6 months old; If the third tooth has two cusps its 1 year and 7 months old. For the rest of its life the third tooth will have two cusps.   Cusps are the number of points on the tooth.

An adult will have 6 incisors and 2 canine in the lower front and 6 pre molars and 6 molars in the back. They will have the same number of molars and pre molars on top for grinding their food. The height of the tooth above the gum line on all 3 molars is used to determine deer age. They lose about 1 millimeter of height each year. If they are where there is sandy soil the teeth will wear down faster. Adult deer have only two peaks on the third cheek tooth. They are aged by the amount of wear on these teeth. About 95 percent of the deer harvested are 3 ½ years or younger. The 2 ½ year old deer have sharp peaks on all of the cheek teeth and very little wear on the last tooth. The 3 ½ year olds begin to show wear on the peaks of the fourth tooth, and the peaks will have a brown center. The last cusp on the rear tooth will be worn into a shallow cup shape.

Very old deer are relatively easy to recognize because all the teeth are worn flat and nearly into the gums. It is the deer between 3 ½ and 6 ½ years which are difficult to age.

Teeth are designed to chew tough food. Deer have incisors in the lower jaw for biting and molars for grinding.

Deer tracks

Deer tracks are heart shaped. The track is made by a deer's hooves also called toe nails. The pointed end points to where the deer is going.

The most reliable indicator of sex and age is the measurement from hoof to dew claw. (Overall length). In soft ground the dew claws will show on bucks and does. It is believed that bucks drag their feet to save energy.

In this picture you can see the marks of the dew claws.

A doe's chest is narrower and her tracks will tend to fall right on top of her front hooves or slightly outside. A buck tends to have a wider chest than hind quarters. His rear tracks will fall to the outside of his front tracks and will often fall short of his front tracks and he toes out slightly.

In this picture you can see the one hoof print on top of the other. This was probably a doe.

A fawn track is 3 to 3 ½ inches from point to dew claw.
A yearling doe is 4 inches.
An adult doe or yearling buck is 4 ½ inch.
A 2 ½ year old buck is 5 inches.
A 3 ½ to 6 ½ year old buck is 5 ½ to 6 inches from point to dew claw.

Deer are cloven hoofed animals. Each hoof has two large toes. They are sharp enough to stomp and slash an enemy. They have heart shaped foot prints. The outer part of the hoof is made of material similar to our fingernails and is kept worn down by the hoof's scraping on the ground as the deer walks.

The soft spongy gray area of a deer's hoof bottom gives it suction for better footing on smooth, rocky or sloping surfaces.

Deer coats

A deer's coat is grayish brown in winter and changes to reddish brown in the summer. This color change keeps deer camouflaged all year.

This shows how they look when they are shedding the winter coat. This is a June picture.

Some of the pictures below will show how well they can blend into their surroundings.

Notice the rich reddish gold color for summer. This is another picture of Timex.

Antlers

Age, nutrition and genetics determine antler size which establishes social status.

The male deer is called a buck. In the summer and fall they grow a set of antlers also called a rack. The rack is made of bone and has points called tines. Many tines on a rack tell us the deer is healthy and lives in a good habitat. Bucks antlers reach full growth in the fall. When he first gets them they are covered with velvet which he rubs off on trees in the fall. The breeding season for the buck starts about the time he sheds his velvet. He becomes less wary and more vulnerable to accidents. He will do things that he usually would avoid. He will act like a headstrong teenager.

He will scent mark his area to advertise his presence to other bucks and to attract does. The antlers are grown and shed each year growing larger each year. Notice the example in the picture. This is the same bucks antlers, starting with the first year at the bottom, then the second year and finally the third year when he died of natural causes. Each year they grow thicker and bigger.

They shed their antlers in January to March after the breeding season and then begin to grow new ones in April or May.
The longer they keep the antlers depends on how well they eat.
The antlers stem from pedicles on the skull.

This shows the rack just starting to form. He is also loosing his winter coat. When a buck is a year old he will begin to grow his first set of antlers, usually a single pointed spike.

They grow fast and reach full size at 12 to 16 weeks. During the growing period they are covered by velvet which is a skin like covering that supplies blood to the antlers as they grow. It has fur covering it. Once fully formed the tissue under the velvet gets solid into what we recognize as antlers. Then the skin or velvet will dry and crack splitting open.

Antlers are not horns, horns are permanent and continue to grow year after year. Antlers are temporary. They begin as knobs. The velvet is actually a network of blood vessels and as they continue to grow more blood is pumped up to nourish them. The deers neck gets thicker and more muscular from the weight of carrying the antlers.

The velvet is no longer needed to supply nutrients to the growing tissue so then they rub it off. He will rub his antlers on bushes and trees gradually removing the velvet. They lose the velvet in August and September. The antlers are white after they loose the velvet covering them. The buck on the left has rubbed his velvet off and the one on the right still has his.

During the mating season called a rut, bucks fight for territory. They will crash antlers to claim territory. They will stomp their feet and make scrapes on the ground and rubs on trees.

The antlers do not serve as weapons, but are used during the mating season to fight other males for breeding rights to the females.

These two bucks have gotten their antlers tangled fighting.

This is a tree that has been shredded by a buck rubbing his antlers to remove the velvet. Notice the shredded bark on the ground.

In some cases large antlers enhance a buck's social rank. You can strike 2 antlers together and that is called a rattle. That will attract other deer if you are hunting... The best place to find antlers is where they have jumped a fence. The jolt of landing will cause them to fall off. You can hunt the antlers in early spring. Insects and other animals will also eat them.

Antlers can be up to 3 feet across. A large buck can be 4 feet tall and weigh up to 300 pounds.

The size and shape of the antlers including the number of points is determined by the quality and quantity of food, genetics and hormones. The number of points is not reliable to determine a buck's age.

This buck has been fighting and broken off one of his antlers. You can see the bloody spot where it was.

A couple of days later, the camera caught him again. He has been fighting again and broken more of his remaining antler off.

Abnormal antlers occur on some bucks and genetics is the biggest cause. The genes that cause unusual racks are passed from one generation to another. The following pictures will show how much they change month to month. They will also show the different forms they will take, each one being unique to that buck

This is a picture taken in May when the antlers are first starting. The buck on the right has an abnormal rack. That means both sides are not the same.

The above picture is of the same deer in June.
 I was amazed at how fast they grew. Notice how slim the body is. The picture below is the same deer in July. He has now completely shed off and his rack is almost full size. I am taking pictures a month apart.

Here is the same buck in September. His rack is fully formed and he has gotten his winter coat. He still has all his velvet, but will be loosing it any day.

This is a July picture of a deer called Timex.

He has an outstanding rack for a three year old buck. It still has more scope for growing.

This is a picture of Timex loosing his velvet. It is hanging like ribbons from his antlers. His neck has gotten thicker and more muscular from the weight of the antlers.

This buck is rubbing off his velvet and has broken off several tips of his antlers. They are brittle and easily broken at this stage.

This is a picture of a button buck on the left. It is this year's fawn and he has the beginning of antlers. He was born this year and has lost his spots when his winter coat came in. He will not actually get antlers this year, just the buttons at the spot where they will form.

Deer Facts

Life span is 9 to 12 years.
Females weigh about 200 pounds
Deer are mostly nocturnal, but can be seen in the day time. They do most of their feeding early morning or when the sun is going down.

These are both bucks, notice the tarsal glands on the hind legs.
Deer will form herds in the winter, but in summer they are in smaller groups. Usually several bucks in one group and a mother with her fawns in another.
Whitetails are ranked as one of the smartest and elusive of all game animals in the world.
Their sense of hearing, sight and smell are amazingly keen.
They are very curious and can get into trouble by investigating strange smells and sounds.
Deer can make sounds.
Fawns can bleat almost like a sheep when looking for their mother.
A hurt or wounded deer will sound like a goat.

All deer will snort when alarmed or to make an unidentified object move. Some will also do it for no reason. It sounds like an explosion of air under pressure. A buck during the rut will make a grunting sound similar to the low grunts that a pig makes.

Tarsal glands

Tarsal glands are the most important gland to whitetails. They are located on the inside of the deer's hind leg. They consist of a tuft of elongated hairs that covers an area of enlarged sebaceous glands. These glands secrete a fatty substance called a lipid that sticks to the long hairs. All deer regardless of sex or size urinate onto the tarsal gland. This is called rub urination. Even fawns less than a month old do it at least once a day. This is probably how their mothers recognize them.

Deer often sniff the tarsal gland of other deer to recognize them.

During breeding season the bucks urinate on to this gland more frequently and don't lick it off. This frequent rub urination along with chemical changes is what stains the gland dark and gives the buck the rutting odor.

Glands on the deer's legs and feet leave a scent on the trail and help to communicate with other deer. A buck marks his territory by removing bark from trees with their antlers. This is called a buck rub. Look for them Sept. to Nov. The scent rubs off on tall grass, weeds or bushes as they walk.

Notice the dark spot on the hind leg, which is the tarsal gland.

The white tail.

The tail is 4 to 10 inches and when alarmed or running will hold it straight up. It is white on the edges and underside. White fur is also located in a band above the nose, around the eyes, inside the large ears, over the chin and throat, on the under belly and the inside of the legs. White tails are used to communicate with other deer. A tail held up means run for cover." When one deer gets scared, they all take off. They use the white tail to wave bye bye.

They also have a very rapid heart beat when they get scared.

Legs

Long powerful legs enable a deer to run up to 40 miles an hour, jump 8 feet fences, 25 feet broad jump and swim 13 miles per hour. They can run 3 miles or more at a speed of 20 miles an hour.

Stomach

A 4 chamber stomach allows deer to digest tough plant foods. Deer eat quickly and barely chew their food. Later as they rest, they cough up their food and chew it. The white tailed deer is a ruminant. Its stomach has four chambers for digesting food. In the first two chambers, the rumen and the reticulum, food is mixed with bile to form the cud. When the deer is resting it will chew its cud. The cud is regurgitated and re-chewed and swallowed. Then it will pass through the rumen to the omasum where water is removed. Finally, the food enters the last chamber, the abomasums, where it is sent on to the small intestine where the nutrients in the food are absorbed. This digestive system lets the white-tailed deer eat foods like woody plants that other animals can't digest. If deer have enough food, water and shelter, their population can grow rapidly.

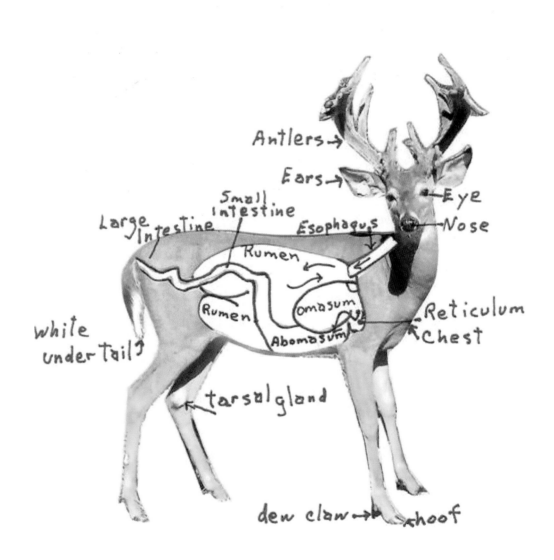

Deer Diet

During the spring and summer, the deer have a lot of choices as to what they will or can eat. The will eat an assortment of leaves, twigs and low growing plants. They eat a lot at this time. In the fall they switch their diet to fallen crops such as acorns and nuts. They love Pawpaw's and will stand on their hind legs and bend the trees over to get them. Winter is more difficult for them to find food. If the habitat is good, the does may continue to gain weight through December while the bucks just try to maintain their weight. During January and February the quality and quantity of food decreases so they have the ability to slow down their metabolism to save energy. If the winter is unusually harsh they can be in serious trouble. Deer feed the heaviest in the early morning or just before dark and if left undisturbed will feed again at noon. If it is hunting season and there are a lot of hunters in the woods, they will stay hidden during the day and only eat at night. If it is a bright moonlit night, they may feed all night and move very little during the day. If bad weather is coming they can sense it and will feed more heavily for 12 to 24 hours before the system gets to them. When the storm hits, they will bed down and wait it out. As soon as the weather gets better they will quickly begin eating to make up for any lost time. When there is light rain and wind, a deer will eat as normal.

Some of the foods that a deer likes to eat are:

Nuts: some of the ones they like are red and white acorns, beechnuts and hickory nuts. Acorns are low in protein, but high in carbohydrates, the best source of energy. If acorns are plentiful the deer will be eating them to put on the extra weight that they need to survive the winter. They prefer the white acorn most of all. It has a sweeter taste than the red acorn.

Plants: non-woody plants are very important to the deer especially during the Fall. Deer graze on grasses, sedges, and ferns. Plants that usually appear after a fire. These areas become very lush and attract a lot of deer. Plants also thrive along roads, forest openings, powerlines and at the edges of fields.

Woody Plants: after the leaves fall from the trees, the deer start eating the woody stems or twigs. Because these have poor nutrition, the deer will eat it only if nothing else is available. Some examples of woody twigs or stems are maples, dogwoods, aspen, blueberry, hemlock, poison ivy, honeysuckle, sumac, poplar and chokecherry.

Mushrooms: deer eat the highly nutritious mushroom as a supplement to their diet. Deer can eat many species that are deadly to man.

Farm Crops: clover, alfalfa, corn, winter wheat, oats, soybeans, peas, sweet potatoes, and apples are a few of the crops eaten by the deer. These crops are very important to the deer after all acorns are eaten. When winter sets in, these may be all that is available to them.

Water: all living things require water to survive. In the winter this may be hard to get, since they require about 1 ½ quarts for every 100 pounds of body weight every day. In the warmer months they need about twice that much water. Although deer will seek out water much of the water that they need can be found in the food that they eat most of which is between 50 and 90 percent water. In the winter they can meet their daily needs by eating snow or by licking ice if open water cannot be found.

Two stories from the woods.

STILL STANDING

By Virginia Hacker

I was formed as a tree, now I am a post placed on end in the ground, anchored by soil. Others followed and formed a row. This will hold a fence, either in or out. Two steel pronged staples hammered in me with a barbed wire. A sharp prong is placed on the top. I have felt many a bird's feet stop and rest. Some have had food in their mouth to feed the young in nearby nests.

Animals grazed in other fields nearby as a mother deer leaps over me. I wonder if this song "Don't Fence Me In" has hurt the longing to roam.

Being of wood, I've always been outdoors through hot summer days with thunder and flashes of lightning close by. Winter howling winds struck me with cold snow flakes that lingered for days, to leave this country scene a silhouette of brown and white objects. Rain turned to ice, coating me, a solid sheet of clear crystal beauty in bright sunlight.

Once a bird deposited a seed that grew clinging on the fence. The next year it bloomed with the most fragrant smell and bore fruit again for the bird. Deer come and nibble on the leaves. Each morning the sun rose on one side and sat on the opposite side as it went down. The moonlight of orange color at harvest time for farmers in October shone brightly.

Airplanes from early open cockpit with 2 wing style to now the jet airplanes. Very, very fast they fly ever so low sweeping warthog style. They are gone before you know it. They come from Peru , Indiana at Grissom Air Base. They are on training mission trips, turning backwards over Andrews (a small town in Indiana) to land in minutes at Peru , Indiana .

Here I stand when people spend days in outer space and return to land on mother earth with me. I am weathered with age watching time go by.

The ghost

The storm clouds were beginning to show up in the sky. Big billowing puffs in the sky. As the darkness was moving in, I could feel the tenseness in the air. The animals always know when a storm is coming. There are changes in the air pressure. I go slowly looking for mushrooms. The rains have been bringing them up.

I have heard the tales the Indians have told of the ghosts in my woods. We used to go ghost hunting at night to see if we could see any. The flickering of the fireflies would light the path as we went.

Now it is still day time, but before a storm the spirits are restless. Today my timing has been right. I sense their presence before I saw the movement. It was just a blur, but the camera is quicker than the eye. This will be something to remember. Maybe someday I will see the old Indian that lives in my woods.

Other books by Martha Philbeck

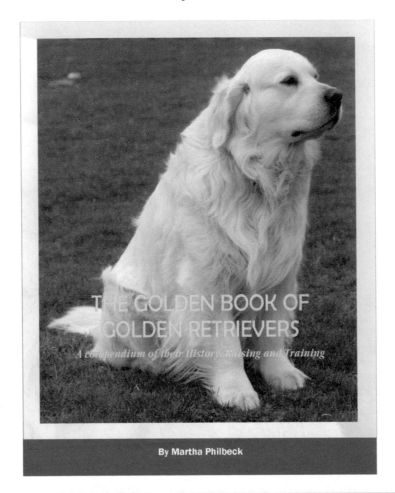

THE GOLDEN BOOK OF GOLDEN RETRIEVERS

A compendium of their History, Raising and Training

By Martha Philbeck

A lovely story of a goose that found it difficult to take off but did not give up. By sheer dint of will power and application he did finally manage to fly; of course, with the help of his father!

The Goose that could not Fly

By Martha Philbeck

Promoted by:
Gunas Publishing
gunaspublishing@yahoo.com

US$

Martha's *Farmhouse Cuisine....*
Martha's Special collection of

Countryside Desserts...
Recipes from the 1900s for the kitchens of 2000s

By Martha Philbeck

Martha's *Farmhouse Cuisine....*
Recipes from the 1900s for the kitchens of 2000s

**Collection of Main Dishes,
Farmhouse Wisdom and much more**

By Martha Philbeck

This is the story in easy steps of the life and family and birth and nurturing of the Canadian goose. In easy to understand language you learn about the habits and needs of the Canadian goose and how to raise the young. Full knowledge about the eggs and their incubation is also included.

THE CANADIAN GOOSE
BY MARTHA PHILBECK

Promoted by
Gunas Publishing
gunaspublishing@yahoo.com

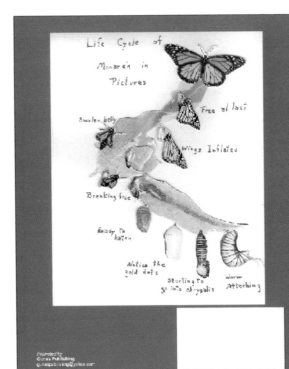

Monarch Butterflies

Messengers of the Great Spirit

Raise them, Release them and Set your wish

By Martha Philbeck

Promoted by
Gunas Publishing
gunaspublishing@yahoo.com

Charlie Coyote and other short stories.

Martha Philbeck & others

WILDLIFE ON MARTHA's FARM

The farm is a place of solace where we can connect with nature and vibrant life.

Pictures and texts by Martha Philbeck.

The cow is our foster mother. It has been supplying us milk all throughout our lives. Where and how this milk is produced and then reaches us is a wonderful story that we should all know. In this book we show you how milk used to be collected 70 years ago and how with science and mechanization, it has been possible to not only increase the yield but also improve hygiene and automate the entire process. See it all in this book in detail through text and pictures.

Different Breeds of Dairy Cows

Guernsey

Holstein

Brown Swiss

Jersey

Milking Shorthorn

Ayrshire

Promoted by
Gunas Publishing
gunaspublishing@yahoo.com

Milk Dairies
70 years ago and now

Pictures, illustration and text by
Martha Philbeck

Isaha and the Donkey
by Martha Philbeck

Hey Grandma
there's a Bird in this Egg

By Martha Philbeck

goldenpaws@embarqmail.com
www.homeofthegoldenpaws.com

Promoted by
Gunas Publishing
gunaspublishing@yahoo.com

Poignant stories by children and for children;
an interesting and heart rending collection.

Charlie Coyote and other stories
Volume 2

Promoted by Gunas Publishing
gunaspublishing@yahoo.com

By Martha Philbeck

Made in the USA
Lexington, KY
09 December 2011